ROBERT
HOOKE

NATURAL PHILOSOPHER AND SCIENTIFIC EXPLORER

SPECIAL LIVES IN HISTORY THAT BECOME

Signature LIVES

ROBERT

HOOKE

NATURAL PHILOSOPHER AND SCIENTIFIC EXPLORER

by Michael Burgan

Content Adviser: Dr. Allan Chapman,
M.A., D. Phil., D. Univ., F.R.A.S.
Wadham College, Oxford University

Reading Adviser: Rosemary G. Palmer, Ph.D.,
Department of Literacy, College of Education,
Boise State University

Compass Point Books ✦ Minneapolis, Minnesota

Compass Point Books
3109 West 50th Street, #115
Minneapolis, MN 55410

Visit Compass Point Books on the Internet at *www.compasspointbooks.com*
or e-mail your request to *custserv@compasspointbooks.com*

Editor: Mari Bolte
Page Production: Bobbie Nuytten
Photo Researcher: Svetlana Zhurkin
Cartographer: XNR Productions, Inc.
Library Consultant: Kathleen Baxter

Art Director: Jaime Martens
Creative Director: Keith Griffin
Editorial Director: Nick Healy
Managing Editor: Catherine Neitge

Library of Congress Cataloging-in-Publication Data
Burgan, Michael.
 Robert Hooke : natural philosopher and scientific explorer / by Michael
Burgan.
   p. cm. — (Signature lives)
 Includes bibliographical references.
 ISBN-13: 978-0-7565-3315-1 (library binding)
 ISBN-10: 0-7565-3315-5 (library binding)
 1. Hooke, Robert, 1635–1703—Juvenile literature. 2. Scientists—Great
Britain—Biography—Juvenile literature. I. Title. II. Series.
 Q143.H7B87 2008
 509.2—dc22
 [B]   2007004904

This book was manufactured with paper containing at least
10 percent post-consumer waste.

Signature Lives

SCIENTIFIC REVOLUTION

The Scientific Revolution was a period of radical change in basic beliefs, thoughts, and ideas. Most historians agree that it began in Europe about 1550 with the publication of Nicolaus Copernicus' astronomical theories about Earth and its place in the universe. It ended about 1700 with the landmark work of Isaac Newton and his resulting universal laws. During those 150 years, ideas about astronomy, biology, and physics, and the very way scientists worked, underwent a grand transformation.

Table of Contents

Robert Hooke
born 1635 dyd 1703
natural philosopher
astronomer
microscopist
physicist
horologist
mechanist
phsyiologist
anatomist
geologist
architect
artist
surveyor

1 STUDYING THE LARGE AND THE SMALL

❧❦❧

When looking out his window, Robert Hooke saw tiny black specks scurrying across the inside panes of glass. The moving dots were mites, common insects of 17th-century London. Hooke was a scientist with a curious mind. He believed everything around him deserved close inspection. To learn more about the tiny intruders in his room, Hooke placed one of the mites under the lens of a simple yet great invention, the microscope.

The first microscope was invented about 1610, 50 years before Hooke noticed the mites on his windowpanes. Hooke, a practical inventor as well as a deep thinker, had come up with improvements for the early microscope. He needed light to closely examine his subjects, so he filled a glass globe with

No original painted portrait of Robert Hooke is known to exist. Artist Rita Greer has used two detailed written descriptions in an attempt to recreate Hooke's face and appearance.

For thousands of years, humans knew that looking at an object through water distorted the object to make it look larger than it was. Later they learned that curved glass lenses had the same effect. In 1608 an inventor named Hans Lipperhey put two lenses in a tube to create the first refracting telescope. The lenses bent light in such a way that objects far away appeared to be closer. He is also given credit for creating the first microscope. While the telescope made distant objects appear closer, the microscope made tiny objects look larger.

salty water. Then he placed an oil lamp near the globe, and used a glass lens to direct its light through the globe. The water in the globe helped strengthen the light.

With such a microscope, Hooke studied various mites, which he later called "little pretty creatures." Over several years, he also studied other insects, including flies. To watch a fly's wings move, he glued a living fly to the end of a feather. Hooke also studied pieces of cloth, plants, the tip of a needle, and the effects of striking a piece of steel with flint (a process that can create a spark). Finally, in 1665, Hooke published the results of his work in a huge book called *Micrographia*.

The book weighed between 2 and 3 pounds (between 0.9 and 1.35 kilograms) and was filled with descriptions of what Hooke saw under the microscope. He stated that his goal was to use "a sincere hand, and a faithful eye, to examine, and to record, the things themselves as they appear." Along with his words, Hooke included stunning, detailed drawings of what he saw under the micro-

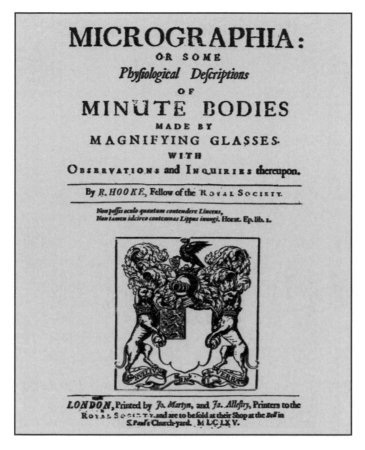

MICROGRAPHIA:

OR SOME

Physiological Descriptions

OF

MINUTE BODIES

MADE BY

MAGNIFYING GLASSES.

WITH

Observations and Inquiries thereupon.

By R. HOOKE, Fellow of the Royal Society.

Non possis oculo quantum contendere Lynceus,
Non tamen idcirco contemnas Lippus inungi. Horat. Ep. lib. 1.

LONDON, Printed by Jo. Martyn, and Ja. Allestry, Printers to the
Royal Society, and are to be sold at their Shop at the Bell in
S. Paul's Church-yard. M DC LX V.

Micrographia *held detailed observations and illustrations of objects Hooke saw under his microscope.*

scope's lens. Like no other scientist of his time, Hooke was a skilled artist. For the first time ever, people could see a world around them that they barely knew existed. His drawings of insects made them seem, he wrote, as if they were lions or elephants seen with the naked eye. Readers also learned about what Hooke called "eels" swimming in vinegar. The creatures were actually nematodes, microscopic worms found all over Earth.

In the pages of *Micrographia*, Hooke made several contributions to science. Studying a cork, he saw many tiny boxlike structures that he called cells. He figured that one cubic inch (16 cubic centimeters) of cork contained 1.2 billion cells, "a thing almost incredible, did not our microscope assure us of it by ocular demonstration." The sections reminded him of tiny rooms, called cells, in which some monks lived and prayed. Hooke was the first scientist to talk about cells in living creatures, though he didn't realize their importance in keeping those creatures alive. That discovery would have to wait until the 19th century.

Hooke's illustrations in Micrographia *included drawings of insects, stones, plant cells, and even his own microscope.*

Hooke did not just study the microscope. At the end of *Micrographia*, he described some observations that he had made using a telescope.

Hooke drew a detailed section of the moon's surface, showing craters, hills, and valleys. He also suggested that the force known as gravity might be at work on the moon, as it is on Earth.

In just this one book, Hooke touched upon many scientific ideas. He explored the nature of color and light, the process of combustion—the act of burning—and the possibility of making artificial silk. He illustrated an improved barometer he had made for measuring air pressure. And he threw out ideas designed to stir other scientists to do their own experiments and observations.

One scientist who read *Micrographia* was Isaac Newton. He scribbled out seven pages of notes on the book, especially the sections on light and color. In the decades to come, Newton and Hooke would some-times exchange letters and ideas. They shared the same goal— understanding the universe. But the two men became rivals, with Newton's ideas often receiving more support than Hooke's. The rivalry turned

Isaac Newton and Hooke became fierce rivals.

personal when Hooke pointed out errors in Newton's work and accused him of stealing his ideas.

After Hooke died, Newton became the most famous English scientist in history, and one still considered a genius today. Hooke, though, was often forgotten. When he was remembered, he was sometimes painted as a bitter man who accused many scientists, not just Newton, of taking credit for work he had done years earlier. But in recent years, historians have tried to show a more complete picture of Hooke. He was not a mathematical genius, as Newton was. But he had a wide range of talents. In addition to his work as an illustrator, he

Hooke's microscope was an important tool in his studies.

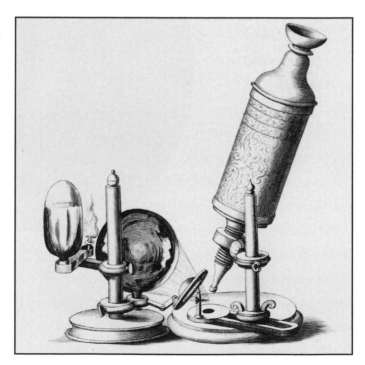

was an architect who designed public and private buildings in London. Hooke also worked in many scientific fields. Today scientists tend to focus on one area of study. His work touched upon physics, chemistry, geology, biology, meteorology, and astronomy. He also knew and worked with some of the greatest scientists of the 17th century, a time when modern methods of science were quickly developing.

By 1667, Hooke was one of the most famous scientists in Europe. He is sometimes called England's Leonardo. The Italian painter Leonardo da Vinci was one of the greatest thinkers of all time. He lived during a period called the Renaissance, a French word meaning "rebirth." Like Hooke, da Vinci was skilled as an artist, scientist, and engineer. Unlike Hooke, the great Italian is widely honored today. But in 2003, the 300th anniversary of Hooke's death, a number of books and papers were released about him, and Hooke finally began to receive more of the credit he deserved for his devotion to science and exploring the natural world. ℘

From about 1300 until 1600, Europeans rediscovered ideas about art and science that had been developed by the ancient Greeks and Romans. This period is often called the Renaissance. Educators tried to make students familiar with all types of science and arts. Such a well-rounded person is known today as a "Renaissance man."

2 ISLAND BOYHOOD

೭ೲ

Robert Hooke's success as a scientist might have surprised his father, who was his first teacher. John Hooke was an Anglican priest and had a solid college education, as most Protestant clergy of the 17th century did. Yet as one of Robert's friends later noted, the elder Hooke "was not mathematical at all," while his son went on to teach geometry, as well as to pursue other scientific interests.

Sometime around 1610, John Hooke settled on the Isle of Wight. This diamond-shaped island sits just off the coast of England, near the port of Southampton. It boasts some of the warmest, sunniest weather in a country known for rainy, dreary days. On the Isle of Wight, Hooke married two times. His first wife died soon after the marriage. In 1622, he

With its fantastic geography, the Isle of Wight proved to be an interesting place for young Robert Hooke to grow up.

The Anglican Church was also called the Church of England. During the 1530s, King Henry VIII battled with the pope, the leader of the Roman Catholic Church. England was Catholic, but Henry wanted a divorce, which was not allowed. He created the Church of England, with himself as its head. The new church became part of the Protestant movement, which challenged the Catholics and the pope. Like his father, Robert Hooke remained an Anglican throughout his life.

married Cecelie Gyles, the daughter of a local merchant. Soon after, the young couple had their first child, Anne. They then settled in the small town of Freshwater, on the island's western end.

Over the next several years, the Hookes had two more children: Katherine, born in 1628, and John, born two years later. Finally, on July 18, 1635, the Hookes had their last child, a boy they named Robert. The family lived in a small cottage, with three bedrooms on the second floor. Most likely, Robert shared a room with his brother, until John left home in 1644 to begin work.

Robert was often sick as a child, and when he was young his parents fed him only milk and fruit. For several years, the Hookes worried that little Robert would not survive, but his health eventually improved. Still, when it came time to begin Robert's education, his parents decided to teach him at home rather than send him to school. John Hooke had already served as a tutor for the son of a wealthy family, so he obviously had a teacher's skills. Frequent headaches, however, made it hard

Homes from Hooke's time still stand on the Isle of Wight.

for Robert to study, and he seems to have ended the lessons with his father around the time he was 7. Still, his learning continued in other ways, fueled by his natural intelligence and curiosity about the world around him.

Surrounded by the sea, Robert seems to have taken an early interest in ships. By watching craftsmen, he learned to work with wood, and during his boyhood, he carved a model ship. As his friend Richard Waller later wrote, Robert "made a ship about a yard long, fitly shaping it, adding its riggings of ropes, pulleys, masts, etc." The toy ship even had small guns that fired. Robert also crafted a clock out of wood, after studying the workings of one made from brass. His power to observe and build would only improve as he got older.

As an adult, Robert Hooke wrote little about his childhood, but it seems that when his health allowed, he enjoyed roaming his home island. He would have seen tall chalk cliffs and worn seaside rocks. He also might have discovered fossils, remains of ancient plants and animals preserved in the soil and rock. As an adult, he came back to the Isle of Wight and found many fossils, which stimulated his thinking about geology.

Robert also showed his artistic skills from an early age. Sometime around 1647, a noted painter named John Hoskins visited the Isle of Wight. According to a friend, Robert watched the master artist and thought, "Why cannot I do so too?" The boy then used natural minerals to make his own drawing materials and copied paintings he saw in his family's house. Hoskins was impressed that a boy with no formal artistic

Fossils are evidence of the plants and animals that lived on Earth millions of years ago. They include shells, dinosaur bones and teeth, branches and leaves, and impressions of animal footprints. The Isle of Wight has been called Dinosaur Isle because so many fossils have been found there. In ancient times, the island's climate supported a large number of dinosaurs. In 1992, a neck bone was found there that was more than 2 feet (60 centimeters) long. The bone belonged to a dinosaur more than 60 feet (18.3 meters) long, the largest ever found in England.

The Isle of Wight offered Hooke an environment open to nature and natural science.

training could paint so well.

Despite his illnesses, Robert's boyhood was mostly pleasant, and his father's career meant the family always had a comfortable life, if not great wealth. But in 1642, troubles in England brought changes to the Hookes. For several years, King Charles I had been quarreling with Parliament, the branch of the English government that made laws. Charles and most of his supporters were Anglican. Many of his opponents in Parliament were Puritans. The Puritans thought the Anglican Church should be reformed. The Puritans also wanted to limit the king's power over the government. The conflict between the two sides erupted into a civil war.

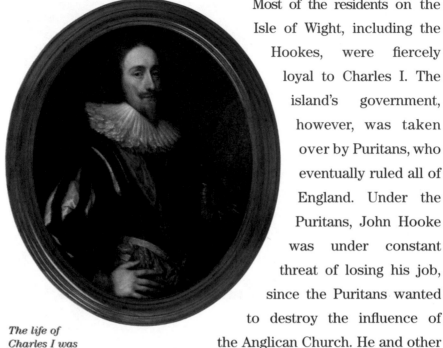

*The life of
Charles I was
surrounded
by controversy
and civil war.*

Most of the residents on the Isle of Wight, including the Hookes, were fiercely loyal to Charles I. The island's government, however, was taken over by Puritans, who eventually ruled all of England. Under the Puritans, John Hooke was under constant threat of losing his job, since the Puritans wanted to destroy the influence of the Anglican Church. He and other Anglicans were also forced to pay higher taxes than the Puritans.

The political turmoil of 1647 reached the Isle of Wight with a particularly dramatic result. That year, Charles' enemies in Parliament held him captive, but he managed to escape. The king fled to the Isle of Wight, where he was warmly greeted. He was technically a prisoner, but the governor of the island let him move about freely. The next year, realizing he had lost the civil war, Charles began talks with the ruling Puritans. He returned to the English mainland and was put on trial. He was executed on January 30, 1649. As an adult, Robert Hooke showed his continuing loyalty to the former king—to honor Charles' memory, on each January 30 he refused to eat.

Charles was still on the Isle of Wight when young Robert was struck by a personal tragedy. His father had been sick for several years, and in October 1648 the clergyman died. In his will, he left Robert "forty pounds (about $6,350 today) of lawful English money, the great and best joined chest, and all my books." Robert also received 10 pounds (about $1,570 today) that his grandmother had earlier left for him when she died. The total of 50 pounds was enough to support Hooke for more than a year.

John Hooke instructed three of his closest friends to make sure his will was carried out. One of them may have helped Robert begin the next phase of his life. Around the time of his father's death—perhaps even before it—the young Hooke left the Isle of Wight and headed for London. There, in England's capital and largest city, Robert Hooke would begin his true education as a scientist. 🦢

In Robert Hooke's time, English currency included pounds, shillings, and pence. Coins were made of gold, silver, and copper, and there were no paper bills. A pound equaled 20 shillings, and one shilling equaled 12 pence. Sometimes foreign coins of gold and silver were also used. The 50 pounds Hooke was given in 1648 was much more than most English workers earned in a year. Some agricultural jobs paid just a few pence per day.

Chapter
3 A KNACK FOR SCIENCE

࿇

When Robert Hooke arrived in London in the fall of
1648, studying science wasn't the first thing on the
13-year-old's mind. He planned to become a painter.
Hooke, or someone he knew, had arranged for him
to serve as an apprentice to Peter Lely, a Dutch artist
working in London. Hooke's time with Lely, however,
didn't last long. With his natural artistic talents,
Hooke thought he could learn to paint on his own.
He also found that chemicals in the artist's paints
worsened his health, so he left Lely.

As with most of Hooke's early life, the details of his
first few months in London are sketchy. But sometime
in 1649, he entered the Westminster School, one of
the oldest and best schools in England. The school's
head was Dr. Richard Busby, and he was impressed

*The Westminster School was founded in 1179, when monks began
teaching poor students who lived near Westminster Abbey.*

with Hooke's quick grasp of ideas. A fellow student later noted that Hooke was rarely seen in classes at the school, leading historians to think that Hooke studied personally with Busby, as well as living in his house. Hooke kept in contact with his first important teacher throughout much of his life.

Richard Busby realized that formal education would not be the best style of learning for Hooke, and instead gave him private lessons.

At Westminster, Hooke studied Euclid, an ancient Greek mathematician who developed a form of geometry named for him. Hooke needed just one week to master the teachings in Euclid's first six

books on geometry. Hooke also learned Greek and Latin. Until the Renaissance, European scholars focused on the works of ancient Greek and Latin scholars, scientists, historians, and artists. Even as new works were written in modern European languages, educated people were expected to read Greek and Latin. Hooke also studied Hebrew, which 17th-century scholars often learned so they could read parts of the Bible originally written in that language. Later in life he also learned French, Dutch, and some Portuguese and Chinese.

Hooke also took time to develop practical skills. He learned how to use a lathe, a machine used to shape wood or metal. With a lathe and smaller hand tools, Hooke would later create some of the scientific measuring devices that he is still famous for. But the many hours he spent at Westminster with the lathe seem to have affected Hooke's body. He blamed that work for back problems he developed, which grew worse as he got older. His friend Richard Waller noted that Hooke's

The Westminster School traces its roots to the 12th century. It was founded as a Catholic school to educate poor students who lived near Westminster Abbey, one of England's most famous churches. Since 1066, almost all of England's rulers have been crowned in the abbey. By the 17th century, the Westminster School was a boarding school for boys. The school is still educating students, and its science center is named for one of its most famous graduates, Robert Hooke.

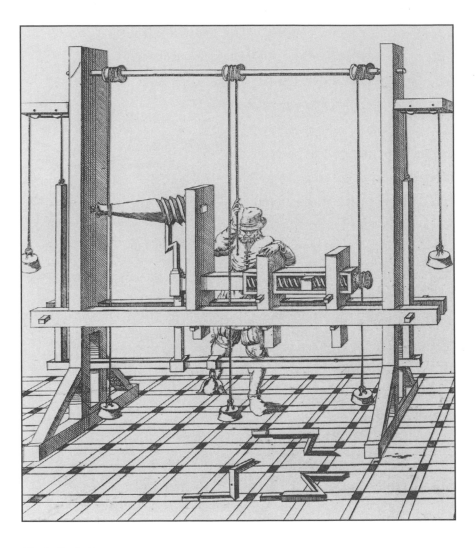

The lathe is the oldest known machine tool, and can be used to shape pottery, cut and sand wood, and make tools that require symmetry.

body was "very crooked."

Although Hooke didn't write or say much about his time at Westminster, he did once claim to a friend that during his four years he discovered "thirty several ways of flying." Hooke didn't offer any proof of this claim, though as an adult he studied the feathers and muscles of birds in his attempt to help humans fly. The claim about his schoolboy work with flying was part of a pattern in Hooke's life. This habit of wild claims led some scientists to dismiss Hooke's work—and to dislike him as a person.

In 1653, Hooke left the Westminster School and went to Oxford University, which was 60 miles (97 kilometers), or two days' travel, from London. Although he took courses and worked with scientists there, he did not formally enroll at the school until 1658. Hooke did not have enough money to attend college on his own, so he worked as a servitor, or attendant. In that position, he did chores for wealthier students. Hooke also played the organ or sang in the choir at the school's church.

At the time, students did not choose one topic as their major, or main area of study. Instead, they were expected to read and understand the great works of a wide range of ancient thinkers, as well as the Bible. The many branches of science known today—including biology, chemistry, and physics— were lumped together under the heading of "natural philosophy." But many of the great thinkers who taught at Oxford had a deep interest in certain areas of natural philosophy. They played a role in creating modern science as it is known today.

Hooke entered Oxford after several major scientific breakthroughs had changed old ways of thinking.

Hooke studied at Christ Church, one of the largest colleges at Oxford University.

For several thousand years, the work of such Greek thinkers as Aristotle, Ptolemy, and Galen influenced natural philosophy. Among other ideas that were later proven false, Aristotle argued that Earth was the center of the universe. Ptolemy used mathematics to show what he thought was true—that the planets and sun rotated around Earth in set patterns. Galen was a doctor who thought human blood was created in the liver, then mixed with air as it passed through the heart.

During the Middle Ages, the roughly 1,000-year period before the Renaissance, the Roman Catholic Church blended the ideas of the Greeks with its own teachings. The notion that Earth was the center of the universe fitted with Catholic teaching that man was God's most important creation. That notion, however, received a jolt with the work of Nicolas Copernicus. In 1543, he published a book that argued—correctly—that Earth and the other planets orbited the sun. The same year, Andreas Vesalius published a book on anatomy with the first accurate drawings of the inside of the human body. His work proved that much of what Galen had taught was wrong. With these new ideas, the so-called Scientific Revolution was beginning.

René Descartes believed that science and math could be used to explain everything found in nature.

By the time Hooke started college, new research was starting to reveal more about the world of nature. Some of this work was influenced by the French philosopher René Descartes. He and his followers tended to start with theories about the world, then look for facts to prove or disprove them. Other scientists stressed observing the world and performing experiments, then using the knowledge obtained to create a theory. England's Francis Bacon was a leading supporter of this approach. Helping the scientists were new tools, such as the telescope, microscope, and the pendulum. For example, Galileo Galilei used a telescope to observe the movement of the stars and planets in an attempt to prove Copernicus' theories.

At Oxford, a group of teachers formed an informal club to discuss the new developments in natural philosophy. Around 1655, Hooke met John Wilkins, one of the leaders of this group. He began aiding Wilkins with experiments. Hooke was already doing similar work with a local doctor interested in neurology. Wilkins became especially important to Hooke's scientific career. In *Micrographia* Hooke gave Wilkins credit for encouraging him to do his own scientific work. He also called the

Like Hooke, Francis Bacon (1561-1626) has been called a Renaissance man. Bacon was a lawyer and writer as well as a scientist. Although he died before Hooke was born, Bacon's ideas influenced the men who taught Hooke. Bacon stressed what is called induction: observing the world, and then using factual evidence to create a general theory that is thought to be always true. Bacon conducted experiments until he died. He wanted to see whether cold could preserve meat, so he stuffed a chicken with snow. Bacon became chilled during the experiment, contracted pneumonia, and died soon after.

Oxford professor "a man born for the good of mankind; and for the honor of his country." Wilkins and fellow club members taught Hooke astronomy, mathematics, and mechanics—the study of energy and forces and their effect on objects. Hooke also credited his mentors with showing him about how force and energy played a part in the movement of pendulums.

Hooke also met Robert Boyle, a wealthy and intelligent Irishman who had been invited to Oxford by Wilkins. Boyle had a deep interest in science, and built his own laboratory in Oxford. Sometime around 1657 he hired Hooke as his assistant. Although Hooke was still just a student, he would play an important role in Boyle's work and would launch his own career in science. ❧

John Wilkins introduced Hooke to fellow scientists who would help his career.

Chapter
4 BEGINNINGS OF A CAREER

❦

By taking the job with Robert Boyle, 22-year-old Robert Hooke did more than make money. Boyle also invited him to live in his home. For about five years, Hooke traveled with Boyle and the two men became lifelong friends. Hooke ran errands for Boyle, wrote some of his letters, and made illustrations for books Boyle published about his scientific work. But Hooke was most useful in the lab, where his mechanical and intellectual skills were on display.

Boyle, like several other members of the Oxford science club, was influenced by the ideas of Francis Bacon. Boyle and the others wanted to conduct experiments to observe and measure the natural world. One notion that intrigued Boyle was a vacuum—the absence of air in a particular space. Aristotle and

Robert Boyle (right) and an assistant performed experiments in Boyle's laboratory.

other Greeks had argued that air, one of the four elements, always filled a space if none of the other elements was present. But in 1643, Italian scientist Evangelista Torricelli created an airless and element-free space, or vacuum, inside the glass tube he used to make a barometer. Other scientists wanted to make larger, more impressive vacuums, where they could conduct experiments. Around 1658 Hooke designed an air pump for Boyle that suited this need.

Hooke's pump had a 15-inch (38 centimeter) glass ball on the top—large enough to hold items that could be studied inside the vacuum. The globe had a lid, which could be opened to place the items inside. A brass plunger, called a piston, moved up and down inside a brass tube called a cylinder, which was attached to the bottom of the globe. The force of the piston moving down the cylinder removed the air from the globe, creating the vacuum. The system was not perfect, since small amounts of air could still seep in around the cylinder and the lid. Hooke used oil at these points to try to keep the pump airtight.

Hooke and Boyle worked together as they pumped out the air and then placed items inside the bulb. They saw that candles went out inside the vacuum. So did glowing coals, but adding air to the chamber made them start to glow again. This work led the men to see that fire was not an element, as Aristotle had argued. The act of combustion, which

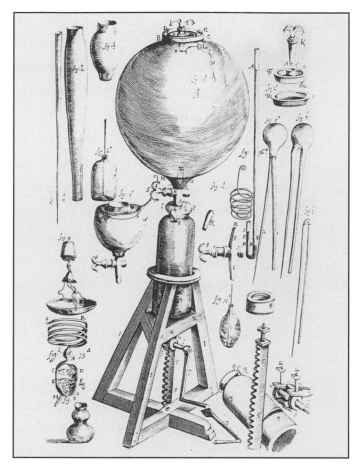

Hooke and Boyle discovered that as the amount of pressure within the vacuum increased, the volume of gas in the vacuum decreased.

started a fire, was a chemical reaction, and air played a role in it.

During his time with Boyle, Hooke also did his own experiments. He was interested in springs and the general idea of elasticity—the ability of a substance that has been stretched to return to its original shape. Hooke saw that springs could be used to make more accurate clocks and watches, a goal of many

At a constant temperature, gas will compress when pressure is applied to it. To scientists, pressure means the amount of weight in a certain area, such as pounds per square inch. Boyle saw that the amount of compression is inversely proportional to the amount of pressure. This means that as the pressure increases a certain amount, the area the gas fills—its volume—decreases by a corresponding amount. For example, if the pressure on the gas doubles, the volume is cut in half. This discovery is called Boyle's Law. Scientists now know that Boyle's Law applies only to gases at low pressures and high temperatures.

scientists and inventors of the era. Keeping accurate time at sea was important to sailors, and the inventor who perfected a reliable sea clock could make a fortune.

Sailors already had tools to tell them their latitude—how far north or south of the equator they were. But they had no reliable way of learning their longitude, their distance east or west from an imaginary straight line between the north and south poles. To determine longitude, the sailors needed to be able to measure how far they had traveled during one hour, and to do that, they needed accurate clocks or watches. But the clocks of the 1650s were not accurate until Christiaan Huygens found a way to use a pendulum to improve them. The pendulum was important because its swings were always perfectly equal for a given length of swing. The regulated motion of the swinging pendulum turned the gears that moved a clock's hands. To achieve this, a device called an escapement made sure the pendulum

Christiaan Huygens invented the first accurate pendulum clock.

released the power of the driving spring through the gears at a steady pace, to keep accurate time.

Huygens built his improved clock in 1656. Within a few years, Hooke was doing his own clock work, though using a spring instead of a pendulum. While a pendulum worked fine in a fixed clock, it stopped on a ship that moved with the ocean. Hooke discovered that a spring expanded and contracted as precisely as a pendulum swung, and had the idea of using a flimsy "hair spring" to control a spinning

> *A pendulum can be anything that hangs from a fixed point and swings freely. As a young man, Galileo noticed that a light hanging on a rope swung back and forth in a regular rhythm, no matter how long the rope was that it hung from. He worked with various pendulums, which convinced him that the speed of the swinging was always constant for a given length. Christiaan Huygens used that knowledge and put short pendulums in clocks. About 15 years later, an inventor named William Clement made a clock with a longer pendulum, which was more accurate than Huygens' clock.*

"balance wheel" escapement that would work even on a ship at sea. The energy was stored in the coiled hair spring, and released in tiny but exact bursts, to control the gears that made the clock's hands move. Hooke's clock was smaller and more accurate than Huygens', he claimed, and would give sailors a better way to find their longitude. The clock also had a new kind of escapement.

Hooke, as he did throughout much of his career, kept the details of his work secret. He later claimed that he discussed his improved clock with several friends, including Robert Boyle. The men were making plans to manufacture and sell the clock, when Hooke changed his mind. He knew "it was easy to vary my principle [in] hundreds of ways" to make similar clocks. Other inventors could copy his idea and make their own timepieces, and Hooke would never see a penny from the sale of them. Hooke's work with clocks and watches would later lead to an argument with

Huygens, when the Dutch scientist tried to sell a spring watch of his own design.

The public battle with Huygens, however, was still many years away. As the 1650s ended, Hooke continued his work with Boyle. He also developed a strong friendship with another talented Oxford student, Christopher Wren. Like Hooke's, Wren's father was a priest, and Wren had often been sick during childhood. Both men also had great artistic and scientific skills. Wren's greatest fame would come as an architect, but his knowledge of math and science matched Hooke's. Throughout his life, Hooke would share ideas and use Wren's insights to improve his own work.

Sir Christopher Wren and Hooke had a lot in common and became close friends.

Like Hooke, Wren was considered a virtuoso—another name at the time for a Renaissance man. And the two men would become important members of the Oxford science club. Wren, who was three years older than Hooke, became a professor of astronomy at London's Gresham College in 1657. Three years later, England saw a great political change that affected many of the Oxford virtuosi. The Puritans were forced from power, and Charles II, the son of Charles I, became king of England. Once again the Anglican Church was England's official church, and royalists—people who had supported the king against the Puritans and his other enemies—received positions of power in the new government. Many of the Oxford scientists were royalists, and the king rewarded their loyalty.

Gresham College became a new meeting place for scientists. In November 1660, some of them gathered to hear Wren lecture. As they often did, they met afterward to discuss science. What the men wanted was a formal club centered on scientific ideas. From this came the Royal Society. Its members, called fellows, met once a week to discuss their latest experiments, which were inspired by the ideas of Francis Bacon. They shared the belief that science should be the result of careful observation of the world, not just theories. Not all of the members were scientists. Some were scholars and politicians who simply wanted to learn more about science. King Charles II gave his support to the group, and he took an interest in some of the society's work.

In November 1662, the group decided to hire someone to do experiments and then report the results. Hooke, with his connection to Boyle and his proven talents, was the first choice. The Royal Society instructed him to "furnish the society every day they meet with three or four considerable experiments." Hooke would take suggestions from members on what experiments to do. But he also had great freedom to do work that reflected his interests in all types of science.

Hooke took the job with no pay. At the time, he was still working for Boyle. The society promised to find income for him, and in 1664 a member came to his aid. Hooke was promised 50 pounds per year for giving a lecture every year at Gresham College. A few months later, the society promised to pay him another 30 pounds (about $5,830 today) per year for his work as curator of experiments. Another source of income was set later in 1665, when Gresham College hired him to teach geometry. Hooke moved to an apartment at the school and lived there the rest of his life. Hooke's career as a scientist was well under way. ✍

The official name of the Royal Society was The Royal Society of London for Improving Natural Knowledge. Although today there are about 1,350 members, originally there were only 12. These original members included John Wilkins, Christopher Wren, and Robert Boyle. The members were called fellows of the Royal Society. New members were elected by existing fellows. Robert Hooke was officially elected a fellow in 1663. Other fellows include Charles Darwin, the famous physicist Stephen Hawking, and Tim Berners-Lee, the inventor of the World Wide Web.

Robert Hooke & Samuel Pepys

5 A WIDE-RANGING MIND

ೞ⌇ಌ

The early 1660s were busy years for Robert Hooke. For a time, he continued to work for Boyle while also carrying out his duties for the Royal Society. His experimental subjects ranged from the oceans to the sky and to the smallest living creatures around him.

In his writings from 1663, Hooke described a device for measuring the depth of ocean water, though he did not build one at the time. A similar device was used in the 19th century to measure the depths of the Atlantic Ocean. He also created a tool that could be used to retrieve samples of ocean water. A bucket with two hinged lids was attached to a weighted rope and dropped into the ocean. Pulling up on the bucket shut the lids. The water trapped inside could then be studied, revealing tiny sea life from the bottom of the ocean.

Robert Hooke began to catch the eye of new members of the Royal Society, including Samuel Pepys (right).

Hooke tried his own diving experiment. He wanted to see whether he could breathe under water, so he copied a trick divers were said to use—putting a sponge soaked in oil in their mouths. Hooke reported, "I was as soon out of breath, as if I had no sponge, nor could I fetch my breath without taking in water." Despite these problems, Hooke kept experimenting with underwater breathing, and later invented a way to send air into a diving bell. These large metal or wooden bells were used by divers to stay under water for long periods.

Diving bells were one of the earliest types of underwater diving equipment. Edmond Halley developed a bell of his own design in the 1690s.

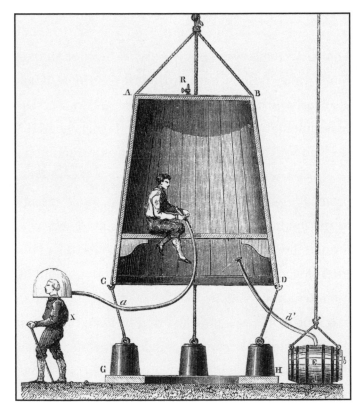

Back on land, Hooke began recording the weather in a detailed way. Taking an idea suggested by his friend Christopher Wren, he began working on what was called a weather clock. The device would automatically record such things as wind speed, temperature, and rainfall. He would need 15 years to design it, and would never build it. He often spent years working on one device, because his wide range of interests led to new ideas and experiments that diverted his attention. Other times, Hooke came up with an idea then abandoned it, leaving other scientists to work on it.

Hooke's interest in measuring the weather led to several achievements. In 1663, he created an improved barometer, an instrument that measures atmospheric pressure and change. Over time, he noticed a relationship between the rising and falling of the pressure and the future weather. As he wrote Robert Boyle, "I ... have found it most certainly to predict rainy and cloudy weather, when it falls very low; and dry and clear weather, when it riseth very high." Hooke later saw that the barometer was not always accurate in predicting the weather. Still, he thought there must be scientific ways to do so—an idea proven with today's meteorology.

Air, to Hooke, was endlessly fascinating. Humans obviously needed air to live, but its properties were still largely unknown. Hooke, through his studies, learned that air played a role in combustion, the act of starting a fire. He also saw that compressed air could create strong forces. In 1664, he invented an air gun. A shot fired from the gun could leave deep dents in solid wood.

The study of air led Hooke to examine respiration—the act of breathing. The English scientist William Harvey had done important early work on the relationship between the circulation of blood and respiration. Hooke wanted to learn even more. For one experiment, he used a live animal as a subject for research, in a process called vivisection. He cut open a dog, put a bellows down its throat, and used the bellows to send air into the animal's lungs. When the air was constant, Hooke saw that the dog's heart beat normally. But when the flow of air stopped, the dog's lungs shrank and the beating became irregular. Hooke recorded his results and presented them to the Royal Society, which wanted him to continue his study. Hooke,

In Hooke's day, vivisection was seen as an acceptable way to learn more about animals. Scientists hoped that learning how the animals' bodies worked would help explain the operation of the human body. Many people believed that God placed animals on Earth to serve humans, and they could not feel pain as humans could. By the 20th century, a movement to stop vivisection had gained strength in England and spread to other nations. Hooke, although he disliked working with live animals, believed that it had some value. The need for using live animals in scientific experiments is still debated today.

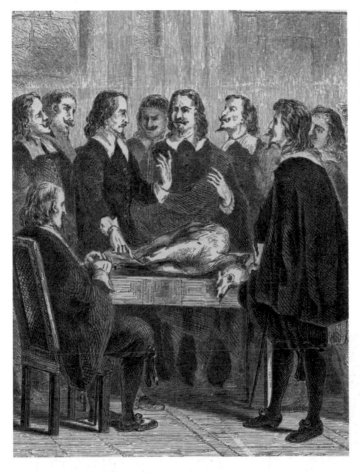

Scientists learned how animals' organs and muscles worked by experimenting on their bodies.

however, put off doing any more. He wrote to Boyle about "the torture of the creature" during the experiment, and he did not want to repeat it on another animal. Hooke did perform other experiments on dead animals, and assisted other scientists with another vivisection.

During 1664 and 1665, Hooke also turned his attention to the skies. He joined Wren, Christiaan Huygens, and several other scientists in observing the movement of a particularly bright comet across the sky. Hooke and the others were benefiting from telescopes much larger and more accurate than the ones Galileo had built several decades before. Hooke had already used one of these telescopes to observe a spot on the surface of Jupiter. He saw the spot move and later said he measured how fast the planet rotated. Hooke did not publicly write about his findings, however, and another scientist received credit for measuring Jupiter's rotation. Hooke's tendency to keep things to himself prevented him from getting credit he deserved. In other situations,

In 1705, Edmond Halley predicted that a comet seen in 1531, 1607, and 1682 would return in 1758. He was right. Halley's Comet was the first recognized reappearing comet. It was last seen in 1986, and will not be seen again until 2061.

Hooke took credit for discovering things but could not prove it. In either case, his methods left other scientists sometimes doubting his word.

With the 1664 comet, Hooke made several observations. He and Wren both suggested that all comets move in a curved or elliptical path, not a straight line. Hooke expressed that idea to the Royal Society in March 1665. Attending that day was Samuel Pepys. He recorded that Hooke said, "This is the very same comet that appeared before in the year 1618, and that in such a time probably it will appear again, which is a very new opinion." In this, Hooke was wrong; the comet of 1664 was not the same as the comet in 1618. But the idea of comets returning was an advanced and far-sighted thought for the time.

For a time in 1665, Hooke had to conduct his work outside of London. A disease known as the bubonic plague swept through the city, and most of the Royal Society fled to safer locations. About 100,000 Londoners who could not

Samuel Pepys (1633—1703) wrote one of the most famous diaries in the English language. Written from 1660 to 1669, the diary fills nine books. Pepys wrote in shorthand, a system of writing that uses symbols instead of letters, which makes it faster to write. Pepys recorded information about the life of Charles II and also gave a detailed look at the private life of a powerful 17th-century Englishman and his social circle. Pepys belonged to the Royal Society, and he mentions Hooke several times in his diary. Later, when Hooke began his own diary, he recorded meetings with Pepys.

afford to leave were eventually killed by the disease. Hooke, along with his former teacher John Wilkins, went to Durdans, the country home of a wealthy man who was friendly with Christopher Wren. Hooke and Wilkins, joined by another member of the Royal Society, worked together on building an improved carriage. John Evelyn, who visited them at the estate, said the three men together also worked on "new rigs for ships, a wheel for one to run races in, and other mechanical inventions."

On his own at Durdans, Hooke spent time working on timepieces and a new quadrant. Sailors and astronomers used quadrants, or quarters of circles with 90-degree angles. They were used to measure the position of stars, which helped determine their latitude. Quadrants could also be used to measure distances on land. Hooke told Robert Boyle that he hoped his new quadrant would be "the most exact instrument, that has yet been made." Hooke kept on his work with quadrants and would continue working with them in years to come.

The quiet life of the country seemed to stir Hooke's already busy mind. He wrote to Boyle that he was considering new theories and experiments on gravity, heat and cold, air pressure, pendulums, sound, and others. He added, "And I doubt not but some few trials will suggest multitudes of others, which I have not yet thought of."

Hooke constructed a quadrant in 1676 that was 10 feet (3 meters) tall.

In October 1665, Hooke took time from his work to go back to his hometown of Freshwater, on the Isle of Wight. His mother, Cecelie, had died that June, but the threat of the plague had kept him from returning then. Hooke went to Freshwater to settle family matters with his brother and sister. On the visit, he explored the beaches and cliffs, finding fossils that shaped his ideas on geology. After this, he went back to Durdans for several months.

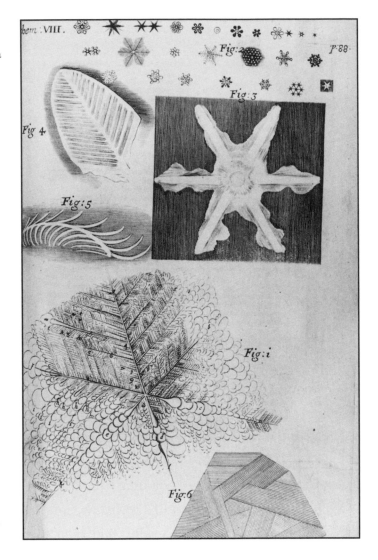

By March 1666, Hooke and most of the other fellows of the Royal Society had returned to London. Hooke's *Micrographia* had been published in early January 1665 and was already winning admirers. The idea for the book had come in 1663, when the society wanted to collect all of Hooke's findings using the microscope. That year, King Charles II had been invited to see some of Hooke's work as curator of experiments, but the king did not show up. The fellows wanted to convince Charles they were doing important work so he would fund further experiments. Natural philosophy was fine for scholars, but the king and other officials wanted to see that the new science had practical benefits. When writing *Micrographia*, Hooke dedicated the book to the king. Calling himself the king's "most humble and most obedient subject and servant," he said he offered Charles "some of the least of all visible things."

There is no record of what Charles thought of Hooke's book. Others, though, were greatly impressed. In his diary, Samuel Pepys called it "the most ingenious book that ever I read in my life." Pepys said Hooke's book made him very proud. Over time, *Micrographia* has been hailed as one of the greatest scientific works ever. By the time of his return to London in 1666, Hooke's reputation as a scientist was assured. ✑

Chapter

6 BUILDING ON HIS FAME

⁙

With the plague over, Robert Hooke returned to his comfortable routines in London. He had his work at Gresham College and his duties as curator for the Royal Society. Now almost 30 years old, Hooke had a rather odd appearance. His back was still crooked, and his friend Richard Waller wrote that he was "always very pale and lean." Later in life, Waller commented, Hooke was "nothing but skin and bones." Another friend noted that Hooke's "head is large, his eye full and popping, and not quick."

When not working, Hooke spent most of his time with his friends, discussing science. Hooke never married, though he had relationships with several of the young women he hired as housekeepers.

In his diary, Samuel Pepys noted several social

Robert Hooke gained additional fame after the Great Fire of London allowed him to show off his architectural skills.

events that both he and Hooke attended. One was a concert at the home of another Royal Society member. Hooke had learned to play the organ when a student at Westminster School, but his interest in music was as much scientific as artistic. Unlike many scientists of the day, he believed that sound was caused by vibrations in the air, which created vibrations inside the ear. Hooke had already learned that a string vibrating at a rate of 272 times per second created the musical note of G. He remained fascinated by the mathematical nature of music, and was ahead of his time in understanding that vibrations in the air created sound.

Hooke also noticed that sounds within the body seemed to indicate a person's health. A fast or slow beating of the heart, for example, could be a sign of illness. Hooke suggested that a device could be used to listen to the body's sounds, an idea that was fulfilled with the development of the stethoscope 150 years later.

Although science and math dominated his thinking, Hooke did take time for pleasure. He seems to have particularly enjoyed the St. Bartholomew Fair, held each year in London. The fair had once been a religious celebration. By the 17th century, it was like a trade show, where merchants sold such things as cloth, candles, glass, and leather goods. Fairgoers could feast on a variety

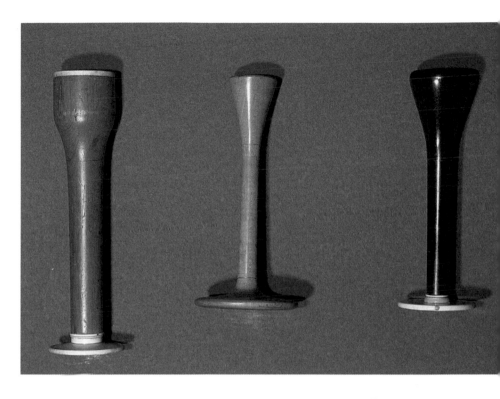

The first true stethoscope was not invented until 1816.

of foods, such as roasted pig, apples, and gingerbread, and children could buy dolls, rattles, and other toys. For entertainment, there were jugglers, singers, plays, and puppet shows. Hooke once wrote about seeing an elephant at the fair "wave colors [flags], shoot a gun, bend and kneel, carry a castle and a man, etc."

In London, Hooke had a busy schedule during the spring and summer of 1666. At meetings of the Royal Society, he discussed some of his theories on gravity. He called it "one of the most universal active principles in the world." Hooke wondered whether gravity's pull was magnetic, electric, or something completely different. In May, Hooke correctly suggested that gravity played a role in the motion of planets around the sun. Hooke, however, did not have the mathematical ability to back up his claim. He also was right in asserting that gravity was stronger near the center of an object such as a planet. He and other scientists would continue to study gravity's relation to the planets and other objects in the decades to come.

With the effects of the plague fading, London was hit with another terrible disaster. On September 2, 1666, a huge fire swept through the city, destroying more than 13,000 homes and buildings. The flames never reached Gresham College, so Hooke was safe, and only five people died in the blaze. But the inner part of London needed to be rebuilt, and quickly. Within days, Hooke had designed a plan for this massive project. He called for the main streets to "lie in an exact straight line, and all other cross streets turning out of them at right angles." Modern historians have noted that Hooke's plans for the city and individual buildings reflected Renaissance thinking. The architects of his age were influenced by the Greeks and Romans. The ancients and the 17th-century men preferred symmetry and geometric shapes in their designs.

Several other Royal Society members, including Christopher Wren, had their own plans for rebuilding

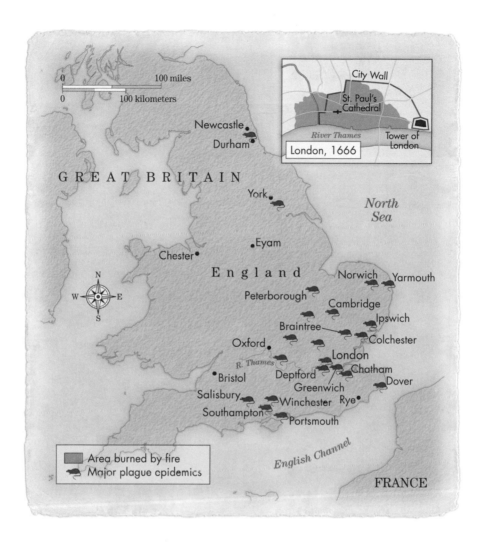

London, 1666

- Area burned by fire
- 🐀 Major plague epidemics

London. Some city officials preferred Hooke's idea, but in the end King Charles and city officials chose six men to work out the rebuilding. The committee included Hooke, who added this new duty to his scientific work.

Helping to rebuild London would prove to be a

Although much of London was destroyed in the Great Fire, only five deaths were documented, in comparison to the 100,000 dead from the plague.

61

> *For hundreds of years, fire was always a danger in London. The city was filled with wooden buildings covered with straw roofs and jammed together. Open flames were common, because people used candles for light and fires for cooking. A fire in 1212 was known as the Great Fire, until the blaze that broke out on September 2, 1666. Burning for four days, this fire destroyed almost 500 acres (202 hectares) in the oldest sections of London. Samuel Pepys recorded some of his impressions on the Great Fire of 1666.*

money-making move for Hooke. In February 1667, Hooke was given the official title of city surveyor, with a salary of 150 pounds (about $29,420 today) per year. He held that position full time through 1673, and did other work for the city in the years that followed. Hooke also collected fees from people who sought his help with building plans. As surveyor, he plotted where streets and buildings would go. He also settled arguments between neighbors who argued over property lines.

The city also used Hooke as an architect. In 1670 he was named an assistant to Wren in the rebuilding of 51 city churches. For centuries after, Wren received most of the credit for designing and building all the churches, but Hooke clearly played an important role building many of them. Several of these churches, historians now believe, were solely Hooke's work, including St. Edmund the King and St. Martin. Hooke also designed a prison and Bethlehem Hospital, a hospital for people with mental illnesses.

Willen Church was another building that Hooke and Wren worked on together. It was built for Dr. Richard Busby, Hooke's old mentor at Westminster School.

Hooke played an important part in building a monument erected to mark the Great Fire of 1666. Once again, Wren is usually given credit for the London Monument, but Hooke's friend John Aubrey said the design was Hooke's. In either case,

Over the centuries, some of Hooke's most famous buildings, such as the Bethlehem Hospital, were torn down. Others, such as the London Monument, still stand. One of the existing buildings is Ragley Hall. Working for a wealthy man named Conway, Hooke began construction in 1680. The large, three-story home took several years to complete. Today the owners, the marquess and marchioness of Hertford, open the home to visitors, so they can admire Hooke's work and the skills of the craftsmen who finished it years later.

Hooke and Wren worked together on the monument, which was finished in 1677. At 202 feet (62 meters) tall, the monument is the world's tallest free-standing stone column. It sits on a spot a distance equal to its height from where the Great Fire was thought to have started. Hooke's influence can be seen in the monument's dual purpose. Although the stone tower was meant to call to mind the fire, it would also serve as a site for scientific experiments. The cellar had a small laboratory, and the roof had a small opening for a telescope. The only experiment Hooke wrote about conducting there involved a barometer. He noted that air pressure fell when the barometer moved from the ground level to the top of the tower.

As Hooke's fame as an architect spread, private groups and citizens gave him business. He designed a new building for the Royal College of Physicians, a job given to him and Wren together, but which he seemed to control. He built homes for several wealthy people, including Robert

Boyle's sister. Despite the money he made from this work, Hooke did not build himself a fine home. Instead, he continued to live in his small apartment at Gresham College. And while his building work went on into the 1690s, Hooke spent less time with it, increasingly devoting himself to his many scientific experiments. ✖

Hooke supervised the construction of more than 30 London churches designed by Wren (left).

65 ✎

7 SCIENTIFIC BATTLES

᭡᭢

Although respected as a great thinker, Robert Hooke could not avoid angering some of the people around him. Hooke's quest to take on new projects meant old ones sometimes lost his attention. As his work as city surveyor went on, some members of the Royal Society complained he was not performing his duties as curator of experiments. The society, however, did not take action against him, perhaps because he was still able to do impressive work.

Through the 1670s, Hooke continued to study some of his favorite topics: light, gravity, and vibrations. A young scientist named Isaac Newton had many of the same scientific interests. Newton, after reading Hooke's *Micrographia*, was inspired to do his own experiments. And like Hooke, he had skills in building tools that would help him observe the universe. Newton built a new kind of telescope, one that used mirrors to send light to the viewer's eye. In 1671, Newton sent this reflecting telescope to the Royal Society. The members compared it with the existing refracting telescopes of the day. They found that Newton's invention, though much smaller, was more powerful in magnifying distant objects. Impressed with the telescope, the society asked Newton to join.

Newton's telescope used mirrors, rather than traditional lenses, to view images.

Hooke, however, did not seem as impressed. He had experimented with smaller reflecting telescopes during the mid-1660s. He considered the refracting scope he built more useful. But now Hooke went to work on building a new reflecting telescope— one that would be better than Newton's. The two scientists were beginning a rivalry that would go on for several decades. At times, they could be friendly to each other. Newton once wrote to Hooke that he succeeded only because of Hooke's work and other scientists before him. Newton's famous words were, "If I have seen further it is by standing on the shoulders of giants." But Newton and Hooke often bitterly disagreed over science, and their feuds became public.

The first disagreement erupted in 1672, after Newton sent the society a paper on color and light. Newton thought that white light contained all the colors of the rainbow. He also said that light was made up of particles. Hooke, in a public letter to the society, dismissed Newton's ideas and promoted his own. Colors, he wrote, appeared only after white light passed through a prism—they did not exist on their own. He believed that red and blue were the basis of all colors, occupying opposite ends of a wave pattern. Greens, oranges, and all other colors fell between red and blue and were created by mixtures, like paints on an artist's palette. And light, Hooke believed, was made of waves. The tone both men took in their writings tended to be insulting, given the polite nature of most public writings in the 17th century. Hooke seemed to dismiss the younger scientist by saying that he had already learned what Newton claimed, "having by many hundreds of trials found them so."

Newton thought Hooke's comments were out of line and made his own jab. He wrote:

> ... he [Hooke] knows well that it is not for one man to prescribe rules to the studies of another, especially not without understanding the grounds on which he proceeds.

In reality, Newton was right about the nature of light and color. A light that seems white is actually made up of all colors. Hooke and Newton were doing what good scientists always do: debating ideas and looking for better explanations. But the personal bitterness between Hooke and Newton never seemed to fade.

Hooke's next scientific dispute came in 1674. He had read the

Light is one of many forms of energy. Similar forms of energy include X-rays, radio waves, and microwaves. Light is the only form of electromagnetic radiation that humans can see. Until the 1920s, scientists saw that light sometimes acted as if it took the shape of waves. Other times it seemed as if it were made of particles. Finally, scientists agreed that light is neither, but it takes on the traits of both, depending on the type of experiment being done to study it. Physicists are still debating the true nature of light.

work of the Polish astronomer Johann Hevelius and disagreed with many of his ideas. Hevelius did not think a telescopic sight could be used with a quadrant to measure the position of objects in the sky. But Hooke had already used a telescopic quadrant that he built to study the comet of 1664. He wrote a book known as the *Animadversion* to attack Hevelius and his ideas. Hooke described an improved quadrant, which featured one of his own inventions, the universal joint. The joint connected two rods that

Newton used prisms to determine the nature of color.

moved in different directions. It let power applied to one rod be transferred to the other. Today universal joints are sometimes called Hooke's joints. They are used in cars and other vehicles to transfer power from the crankshaft, which is turned by the engine, to the axle and wheels.

Hooke's book upset Hevelius, who was also a member of the Royal Society. He refused to accept that telescopic quadrants were better than ones that used the naked eye. He attacked Hooke for claiming he had great ideas but not taking the time to build his

Johann Hevelius became another of Hooke's critics and rivals.

inventions or prove his theories. The Royal Society tried to end the dispute in 1679. It sent Edmond Halley, the discoverer of Halley's Comet, to Hevelius' observatory in Danzig, in what is now Poland. Halley used a telescopic quadrant, while Hevelius used just his eye. The results were almost the same with either method, but Halley, Hooke, and others remained convinced that telescopic quadrants were the best. Hevelius lost support for his traditional method of measuring the skies.

While the disagreement with Hevelius went on, Hooke engaged in a bitter feud with Christiaan Huygens. In the early 1660s Huygens had built a pump he claimed was better than the one Hooke had built for Robert Boyle. Hooke naturally asserted his was better. Later Huygens, like Hooke, wanted to solve the problem of measuring longitude at sea. After his earlier work with pendulum clocks, Huygens turned to springs, as Hooke had done more than a decade before. The two men had earlier confronted each other over the design of air pumps. Now they would battle over who had designed the first practical hair spring balance-controlled watch.

In February 1675, Huygens wrote that he had perfected a pocket watch that used a very delicate spiral spring to keep more accurate time. He recruited the Royal Society's secretary, Henry Oldenburg, to help him get a patent in England for the invention. When Hooke learned this, he was furious on two counts. First, he claimed that he had designed a similar watch and had shown it to the society in the 1660s. And several friends knew that he had considered making and selling his watch, then decided against it. Second, he felt that Oldenburg was secretly working against him to help Huygens. In private, he referred to the secretary as a "lying dog,"

London was a city where Hooke found both support and competition.

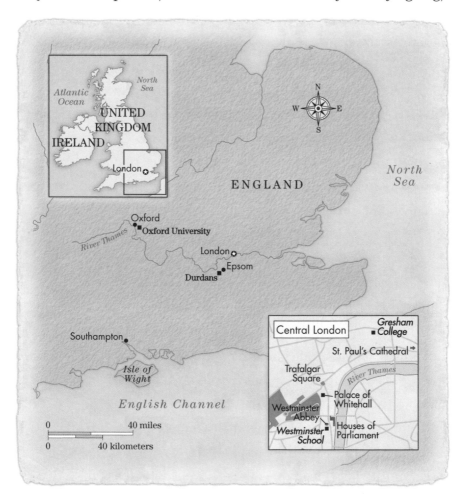

among other unpleasant names.

Hooke quickly found a skilled watchmaker who could build his design. Hooke was now in a race with Huygens to create a watch worthy of a patent from King Charles II. In April, he took one model of the watch to the king. Hooke wrote that the king was "most graciously pleased with it and commended it far above Zulichems [the home-town of the Huygens family in Holland]." But this watch, and others that came after it, lost time and had other problems, which forced Hooke to keep improving his design. In the end, neither scientist won a patent, though Hooke built watches for his friends that seemed to work well. And neither he nor Huygens was able to solve the longitude problem. The first accurate clock for sea travel, designed by John Harrison, did not appear for almost another 100 years.

Hooke recorded some of the details of his watch in his diary, which he had started keeping in 1672. Until then, the glimpses of his life outside the lab came mostly from the writings of others. Now Hooke set down his own observations on both his work and his private experiences. He recorded the weather, his health, and his diet. The foods he ate included eggs, pigeon, and cheese, and his favorite drinks included boiled milk, alcohol, hot chocolate, and coffee. Hooke recorded many visits to local coffee houses, where

Coffee houses began appearing in London around 1650. The coffee beans usually came from Turkey. Coffee was first grown in Ethiopia, where people noticed that eating the beans boosted their energy. Arab traders brought the beans to the Middle East, where people roasted them and mixed them with water to make the first coffee drink. The first coffee houses opened sometime around 1475. Hooke and other 17th-century scientists may have preferred to drink coffee over alcohol when they met in public. They could drink coffee for hours and still be stimulated enough to talk to each other about science.

he spent hours with his friends discussing science.

As in his childhood, Hooke struggled to stay healthy. His diary contains notes about colds, headaches, fevers, depression, and aches. He tried any medicine that friends would suggest. These included various chemicals, plants, and the drug laudanum, which is a form of opium. In one diary entry, Hooke recorded that he was "strangely refreshed" after taking a drug called ammonium chloride and some weak beer. In another he described vomiting five or six times after trying another drug. "I hope that this will dissolve that viscous slime that hath so much tormented me in my stomach and guts." Some modern historians think Hooke may have been a hypochondriac—a person who thinks he is constantly sick when he is not. Some of his ailments also could have been from lack of sleep and stress, since Hooke forced himself to do so much on a typical day.

Hooke's diary also noted some of the people who shared his apartment at Gresham College. They include Nell Young, who served as a housekeeper for him for several years, his niece Grace, and a cousin named Tom Giles. Starting in January 1673, Hooke took on an assistant named Harry Hunt, who worked with him for several decades. Despite his many work demands, Hooke seemed to find time for all the important people in his life, and enjoyed the hours he spent with friends. If those moments also included talk of natural philosophy, Hooke was especially pleased. ℘

Hooke's diary kept careful record of his home and social life.

8 NEW CHALLENGES

❧❧❧

The next decade or so included both highs and lows for Robert Hooke, who was driven to make sure his accomplishments were known. In September 1677, Royal Society secretary Henry Oldenburg died. Hooke had seen Oldenberg as an enemy for some time. Hooke believed that the secretary did not always record his work with the society, so he didn't get the credit he deserved. Within a few months of Oldenberg's death, Hooke was named co-secretary, giving him power to decide what was included in the society's official notes. Over the next few years, however, some fellows criticized Hooke for not writing about the work of other scientists.

Two deaths of people close to Hooke quickly followed Oldenberg's. Hooke's cousin Tom Giles also

Robert Hooke continued to think of new inventions, including a portable "darkroom" for copying landscapes.

died in September, and the following February, he learned that his brother John had killed himself. John Hooke ran a grocery store on the Isle of Wight. Over the years, the business struggled, and Robert Hooke had loaned his brother money during tough times. John Hooke owed money to several people, and he seemed to suffer from depression, just as his brother sometimes did.

Despite the personal losses, Robert Hooke filled his days with work. He continued to perfect a weather clock, he worked on the design of several buildings, and he returned to the microscope, looking for tiny creatures in water. He also wrote about his theory of springs, which was published in 1679. Hooke had often studied springs, as his work with the watches showed. He was interested in the effect of tension, or force, on materials. Hooke had discovered a relationship between the weight attached to a spring and how far the spring was pulled. The force required to return a spring to its original position is in proportion to the distance it moved. This idea was later called

Religious teachings said that God commanded humans not to kill, and Christian rulers used that to make suicide a crime. The punishment for suicide was burying the "criminal" by the road, not in a cemetery, after driving a stake through the body. The suicide victim's money and goods were given to the king, rather than to any surviving relatives. Robert Hooke asked King Charles II to have mercy on his brother's family. The king decided that John Hooke's wife and daughter would receive the estate. Charles also let the Hookes give John a private burial.

Hooke's Law, and it is still used by engineers today. The law, however, does not apply to all materials under all conditions.

Hooke first described his theory using an anagram, in which seemingly random letters can be rearranged to create words. Announcing theories through anagram was not merely a way to conceal discovery. It was also a popular game among scholars, including Hooke, who wrote his anagram as "ceiiinosssttuv." These letters formed the Latin words *ut tensio sic vis*, which mean, *as the extension, so the force*. In this way, he could claim he had a new idea and publicly discuss it, without giving away any details. Hooke wanted to make sure others didn't try to take credit for his ideas. That issue would come up during the 1680s, when Hooke once again had a public squabble with Isaac Newton.

Since his argument with Hooke in 1672, Newton had stopped writing to the Royal Society. Hooke, as secretary, was supposed to make contact with distant members, and in November 1679 he wrote to Newton, trying to improve their relationship. Hooke wrote, "Difference in opinion if such there be me thinks should not be the occasion of enmity [hatred]." The two men wrote a series of letters, mostly about celestial bodies and the nature of gravity. In one letter, Newton made a mistake—he drew a diagram that showed a dropped object moving in a spiral. Hooke corrected Newton and pointed out that the object would travel in an elliptical path. Hooke then angered Newton by pointing out the error to the Royal Society, after Hooke had promised not to talk about their letters in public.

In another of his letters, Hooke tossed out an idea about gravity, based on his own observations and the work of an earlier scientist, Johannes Kepler. Hooke thought there was a relationship between the force of gravity and the distance an object is from the center of a body that pulls on it. The force, he calculated, was in an inverse relationship to the

Planets and stars were only two of the things Hooke and Newton discussed and debated.

distance multiplied by itself. This notion is called the inverse-square law. Hooke did not have the mathematical proof to back his claim about gravity, but Newton took the idea and began to work intensely

to find such a proof. He didn't tell Hooke this, though, and Hooke would not learn about Newton's efforts until several years later.

During those years, Hooke took on a wide range of projects, as usual, with his architectural work an important concern. He also lectured several times on light, and led discussions on scientific theories. For the Royal Society, he carried out new experiments, but his work as secretary was still sometimes weak. In 1682, the society fired him from the job. Hooke's long relationship with the society took another blow the next year. He had to share the curator's job with two other fellows, and his experiments were sometimes kept out of the weekly meetings. The Royal Society also gave him only weak support as he battled to collect money he was owed. Hooke, as promised, had delivered a yearly lecture, but he had not been paid for almost a decade. Then, in 1684, the society ended Hooke's yearly salary as curator. He would only be paid for each experiment he reported on to the fellows. On many fronts, it seemed Hooke could not gain the respect he believed he had earned.

The next blow to Hooke's pride came in 1686, when Isaac Newton published his great work, *Philosophiae Naturalis Principia Mathematica*. In it, he offered a new mathematical proof for the inverse-square law. Newton sent his new work to the Royal Society, which saw its scientific significance.

Philosophiae
Naturalis
Principia
Mathematica
*showed off
Newton's
scientific
genius.*

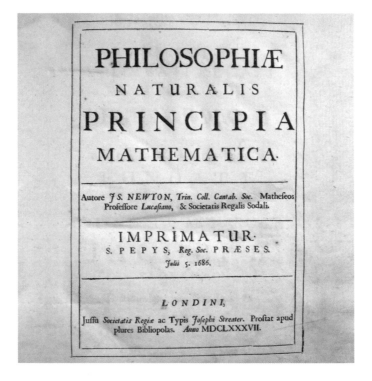

PHILOSOPHIÆ
NATURALIS
PRINCIPIA
MATHEMATICA.

Autore *JS. NEWTON*, *Trin. Coll. Cantab. Soc.* Matheseos
Professore *Lucasiano*, & Societatis Regalis Sodali.

IMPRIMATUR·
S. PEPYS, *Reg. Soc.* PRÆSES.
Julii 5. 1686.

LONDINI,
Jussu *Societatis Regiæ* ac Typis *Josephi Streater*. Prostat apud
plures Bibliopolas. *Anno* MDCLXXXVII.

The society was eager to publish the work, but there
was one small problem. When the *Principia* was discussed at a Royal Society meeting, Hooke was quick
to tell the members that he had first come up with the
proof and had suggested it to Newton. According to
what Newton later heard from some fellows, Hooke
demanded "that he had justice done him." He wanted
Newton to give him credit in the book for suggest-
ing the law to Newton. At first, Newton considered
doing this, but then he grew angry, thinking Hooke
was trying to share in his success. Newton, as the
creative mathematician, had "done all the business,"

and now "another that does nothing but pretend and grasp at all things must carry away all the invention." Newton refused to give Hooke the credit he wanted at the beginning of the book. Some have suggested that Newton even destroyed Hooke's portrait in an attempt to erase his rival from history.

Newton's reaction angered Hooke. So did the praise Newton was winning for his work. But other fellows pointed out that Hooke was partly to blame. He had never publicly written about the inverse-square law, though he had lectured on it in 1682. For the rest of his life, he continued to assert that he, not Newton, deserved credit for the inverse-square law. To some historians of science, this battle between Hooke and Newton was the most distinguishing part of Hooke's life. It seemed to show him, as one historian put it, as "vain, bad-tempered, [and] quarrelsome." The war of words between the two scientists took attention away from all the great accomplishments Hooke had

Newton proclaimed three scientific laws of motion in his book the Principia:

1. An object at rest remains at rest unless some force acts on it. Once in motion, an object remains in motion until a force acts on it.

2. An object moves in the direction in which it is pushed, and the harder the push, the faster the object goes. The larger the object, the more force is required to move it.

3. For every action, there is an equal and opposite reaction. When a force affects an object, the object reacts with equal and opposite force on whatever created the original force.

in so many fields, and perhaps made some people overlook his work.

Hooke, however, did not let the quarrel with Newton stop him from working. In 1686 and 1687 he gave lectures on fossils. Most people of the day thought petrified wood or shell fossils were tricks of nature. Somehow nature copied the shapes of living things and created them in rock form. In *Micrographia*, Hooke had pointed out that petrified wood had the same kind of cell structure as real wood. The hardened wood was not a copy of the real thing. Instead, he said, it was real wood that had

Hooke proved that petrified wood was a result of time and nature.

become petrified over time. Shell fossils, too, Hooke believed, had once been part of real sea life.

Earth and the life on it was always changing,

Hooke believed. He said in a later lecture,

> *There may have been … many … species in former ages of the world that may not be in being at the present, and many variations of those species now, which may not have had a being in former times.*

This thought almost seems to suggest the idea of evolution, which Charles Darwin developed 250 years later. Darwin said that life on Earth had developed and evolved, rather than always remaining the same. Hooke believed that God created all life on Earth, but he could not accept the religious idea that the flood described in the Bible shaped all of Earth's geology. Other forces, such as earthquakes, explained why Earth looked the way it did, he said.

During the time Hooke was lecturing on geology, he suffered a great personal loss. In 1687 his niece Grace died. She had been the most important woman in his life since his mother died more than 20 years earlier. For most of the previous 15 years, Grace had lived with Hooke at Gresham College.

Hooke's friend Richard Waller wrote that after Grace's death, Hooke changed. From that time, he was "observed … to grow less active, more melancholy [sad], and cynical."

Chapter 9

THE LAST YEARS

The year after Grace Hooke's death, England faced difficult political times. King James II had taken power in 1685, after the death of his brother Charles II. James was a Roman Catholic, and he tried to promote his faith through the government. His actions upset powerful Protestants in Parliament, and they prepared to launch a campaign to curtail James' power, including the use of force, if necessary.

Robert Hooke was once again keeping a diary, after stopping for several years. In it, he noted the unsettled nature of the times. Going out to his favorite coffee shops, he sought out reports on the possibility of another civil war. The English Protestants invited the Dutch prince William of Orange to become king. William was the husband of Mary Stuart, the

Robert Hooke continued to write in his diary and remained involved in the scientific community.

89

One drug that interested Hooke was a substance the Portuguese called bangue. Hooke explained the drug's effects to the Royal Society. In his lecture, Hooke gave the first detailed description in English of what today is called cannabis or marijuana. He encouraged further study of bangue as a medicine. Today marijuana possession is illegal in many nations, but some doctors are studying its uses in medicine. Certain chemicals in it seem to eliminate some muscle problems and reduce vomiting. But smoking marijuana raises the risk of lung problems, and it might cause mental health problems. The drug can also reduce a person's ability to make good decisions.

daughter of James II and his Protestant first wife. In one diary entry, Hooke wrote, "Dutch seen off the Isle of Wight." A few days later, he noted that James II had fled and "tis not yet known whither [where] he is gone." When the issue was finally settled without a war and William was in control, Hooke wrote, "God be praised." This bloodless change in government was soon called the Glorious Revolution.

The political troubles didn't seem to keep Hooke from his work, but his health did. Through 1688, he suffered headaches and fainting spells. Richard Waller later noted that the illnesses made it hard for Hooke to work, and Hooke sometimes commented that he lost his vision for short times. He was still trying a variety of herbs, minerals, and other drugs to strengthen his health.

Still, Hooke tried to stay as active as possible. In 1689 he was hired to design a private school and two homes. He also continued to give lectures on science at Gresham College and the Royal Society. His topics covered some of his favorite subjects of the past: optics, fossils, and gravity. Hooke also continued to defend himself from charges that he had never done as much as he claimed. In one lecture, he said he had "the misfortune … not to be understood by some

Gresham College was founded in 1597 and has provided free public lectures for more than 400 years.

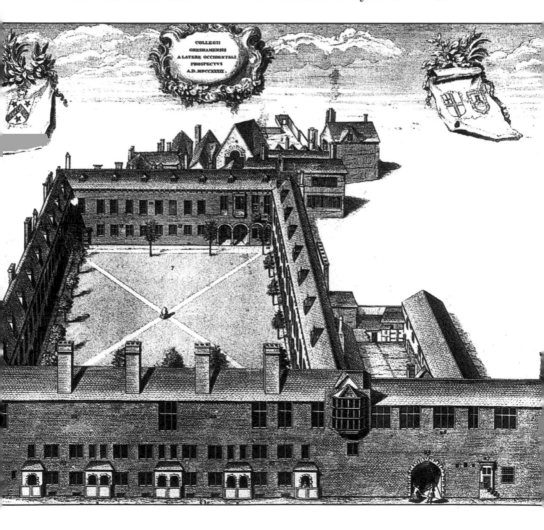

who have asserted I have done nothing," and that "many of the things I have first discovered could not find acceptance." Still, friends such as John Aubrey marveled at all Hooke did, insisting his inventions numbered several hundred. And in 1691, Hooke was given the degree as doctor of medicine, a reward for his many accomplishments.

In his later years, Hooke also kept up with his friends. He met with Christopher Wren and others to discuss new scientific ideas and propose experiments. And he was still active with the Royal Society, even if he was no longer getting paid for any of his services. Although Hooke had made enemies over the years at the society, the fellows realized his many achievements. In 1696 the society offered to pay him to write a complete report of all he had done for the society over more than 30 years of hard work. But, as Richard Waller put it, "by reason of his increasing weakness and a general decay, he was absolutely unable to perform it."

Over the next several years,

One of Hooke's last inventions was a device that helped people draw. He altered an invention called a camera obscura to make it portable. A person wore a wooden box over his head. Light entered the box through a tiny hole and projected an image onto a piece of paper. By tracing the image, the wearer could then make an accurate drawing of the image. Hooke demonstrated the box to the Royal Society in 1695. He thought sailors could use it to draw foreign coastlines or objects they found on their journeys. Similar camera obscuras were used during the 18th century.

Hooke's health continued to fail. His body was thinner and more stooped than ever, and his eyesight continued to weaken. His legs became swollen and stiff, making it hard for him to walk. Still, Hooke managed to get out of his apartment a few times and give lectures. And his mind remained sharp until shortly before his death.

Richard Waller saw Hooke in his final months. He recorded that the old scientist "lived a dying life for a considerable time." As the end neared, Hooke did not change his clothes or wash himself. Hooke died in his apartment on March 3, 1703. Fellows of the Royal Society attended his funeral, which one guest called "noble."

During his last years, Hooke had spent little money on himself, and people might have assumed he was poor. Instead, his friends learned after his death that he had stashed away a small fortune in his home. Inside a chest were gold, silver, and other valuables worth 8,000 pounds (about $1.6 million today). Hooke also owned a small piece of land on the Isle of Wight. And among his most prized possessions were his books. His rooms at Gresham College were filled with 5,000 titles.

In 1697 Hooke had started to write his life story. Perhaps it was one more attempt to make sure the world knew about everything he had done. Waller used those few pages and some of Hooke's

Richard Waller dedicated his publication of The Posthumous Works of Dr. Robert Hooke *to Isaac Newton.*

TO

Sir *ISAAC NEWTON*, Kt.

PRESIDENT,

And to the

Council and Fellows

OF THE

ROYAL SOCIETY

OF

LONDON,

FOR THE

Advancement of *Natural Knowledge.*

THESE

POSTHUMOUS WORKS

OF

Dr. Robert Hooke

Are humbly Dedicated

By *Richard Waller*, S. R. Secr.

scientific papers to write a biography of the famed virtuoso. Waller's collection of Hooke's papers appeared in 1705. By then, Isaac Newton had been elected president of the Royal Society. He had mostly stayed away from the society until Hooke's death, a sign that the bitter relationship between the two scientists had not faded. Newton's fame would only rise, publishing a new version of his *Principia* in English (the original was in Latin). Hooke, however, faded into history.

Today Hooke has reclaimed his place as one of the great scientists of the 17th century. He helped show the value of doing experiments to find scientific truth. His inventions made life easier for astronomers and sailors and inspired future engineers to improve on his designs. Hooke thought everything in the universe should be studied and measured, to increase human understanding. People with such a wide range of skills and interests are rare in any age. ❧

HOOKE'S LIFE

1635

Born July 18 in
Freshwater, on the
Isle of Wight, England

1648

Arrives in
London

1649

Enters Westminster
School

1635

1636

Harvard College founded at
Cambridge, Massachusetts,
the first college in the
English-speaking American
colonies

1646

Blaise Pascal
invents the syringe

1649

King Charles I
of England is
overthrown by
radical Protestants
and beheaded

WORLD EVENTS

1653

Enters Oxford
University

1655

Begins working
with John Wilkins

1658

Builds an improved air
pump for Robert Boyle
and helps him with
experiments on vacuums;
does experiments with
springs and their use
in clocks

1655

1653

Oliver Cromwell
dissolves the British
Parliament and
takes the title of
Lord Protector to
rule as a dictator

1655

Christiaan Huygens
discovers the rings
of Saturn

HOOKE'S LIFE

1663
Decides not to tell the public about his invention of a spring clock

1664
Cuts open a living dog to study its lungs and heart; agrees to give an annual lecture for a fee of 50 pounds

1662
Becomes curator of experiments for the Royal Society

1660

1661
First modern bank notes issued in Stockholm, Sweden

1664
England seizes New Amsterdam from the Dutch and changes the name to New York

WORLD EVENTS

1665

Publishes *Micrographia*; describes the curved orbit of a comet; becomes professor of geometry at Gresham College

1666

Prepares plans for rebuilding London after the Great Fire

1667

Named city surveyor of London

1665

1665

The Great Plague begins in London; 100,000 people will die

1667

John Milton publishes *Paradise Lost*

HOOKE'S LIFE

1672

Disagrees with Isaac
Newton about the
nature of light
and color

1674

Writes *Animadversion*
to discuss his
disagreements with
Johann Hevelius
about quadrants

1675

Announces he had
earlier invented a
spring watch, but fails
to get a patent for it

1670

1670

The Hudson's Bay
Company is founded

1673

Father Jacques
Marquette and Louis
Joliet explore the
Mississippi River and
the Great Lakes

1675

King Philip's War is
fought between the
Wampanoag and
British colonists in
North America

WORLD EVENTS

1691

Receives degree of
doctor of medicine

1695

Demonstrates his
portable picture box
to the Royal Society

1703

Dies March 3 in
London, England

1695

1692

Witchcraft trials
take place in Salem,
Massachusetts; 19
people are hanged

1696

Denis Papin,
a French
mathematician
and inventor,
builds two
submarines

1702

First daily newspaper,
The Daily Courant, is
published in London

DATE OF BIRTH: July 18, 1635

BIRTHPLACE: Freshwater, Isle of Wight,
England

FATHER: John Hooke (?–1648)

MOTHER: Cecelie Hooke (?–1665)

EDUCATION: Westminster School,
Oxford University

DATE OF DEATH: March 3, 1703

PLACE OF BURIAL: St. Helen's, Bishopsgate,
London, England

FURTHER READING

Boerst, William J. *Isaac Newton: Organizing the Universe.* Greensboro, N.C.: Morgan Reynolds Publishing, 2004.

Doak, Robin S. *The Telescope and the Microscope.* Milwaukee: World Almanac Library, 2005.

Langley, Andrew. *Da Vinci and His Times.* New York: DK, 2006.

Shields, Charles J. *The Great Plague and Fire of London.* Philadelphia: Chelsea House Publishers, 2002.

Spangenburg, Ray, and Diane Kit Moser. *The Birth of Science: Ancient Times to 1699.* New York: Facts on File, 2004.

Tiner, John Hudson. *100 Scientists Who Changed the World.* Milwaukee: World Almanac Library, 2003.

Wills, Susan. *Astronomy: Looking at the Stars.* Minneapolis: Oliver Press, 2001.

LOOK FOR MORE SIGNATURE LIVES BOOKS ABOUT THIS ERA:

Tycho Brahe: *Pioneer of Astronomy*

Nicolaus Copernicus: *Father of Modern Astronomy*

Galileo: *Astronomer and Physicist*

Gerardus Mercator: *Father of Modern Mapmaking*

Isaac Newton: *Brilliant Mathematician and Scientist*

On the Web

For more information on Robert Hooke, use FactHound.

1. Go to *www.facthound.com*
2. Type in this book ID: 0756533155
3. Click on the *Fetch It* button.

FactHound will fetch the best Web sites for you.

Historic Sites

The Royal Society
6-9 Carlton House Terrace
London SW1Y 5AG
Library and tour concentrating on the history and achievements of the society and its fellows over four centuries

Great Fire of London Monument
Monument Street, London EC2
Monument commemorating the 1666 Fire of London

barometer
device used to measure air pressure

celestial
relating to the stars and the sky

curator
person in charge of a place that displays exhibits

elliptical
shaped like an oval

grafted
attached by surgery or other special means

ocular
relating to the eyes

opium
pain-killing drug produced from the poppy plant

prism
solid, transparent object that can break up a ray of light into the colors of the rainbow

refracting
the ability to bend light so images can be viewed

symmetry
perfectly balanced along a center line

virtuoso
person highly skilled in the arts or sciences

vivisection
the cutting open of a living creature to study how its body functions

Source Notes

Chapter 1

Page 10, line 8: Robert Hooke. *Micrographia*. CD-Rom Edition. Palo Alto, Calif.: Octavio, 1998, p. 205.

Page 10, line 25: Ibid., preface.

Page 12, line 5: Ibid., p. 114.

Chapter 2

Page 17, line 6: Allan Chapman. *England's Leonardo: Robert Hooke and the Seventeenth-Century Scientific Revolution*. Bristol, England: Institute of Physics Publishing, 2005, p. 4.

Page 19, line 10: Lisa Jardine. *The Curious Life of Robert Hooke: The Man who Measured London*. New York: HarperCollins, 2004, p. 29.

Page 20, line 22: Stephen Inwood. *The Forgotten Genius: The Biography of Robert Hooke 1635-1703*. San Francisco: MacAdam/Cage, 2003, p. 7.

Page 23, line 8: *The Curious Life of Robert Hooke*, p. 53.

Chapter 3

Page 28, line 1: *England's Leonardo*, p. 2.

Page 28, line 4: Ibid., p. 8.

Page 33, line 1: *Micrographia*, preface.

Chapter 4

Page 40, line 21: *The Forgotten Genius*, p. 32.

Page 43, line 3: Adrian Tinniswood. *His Invention so Fertile: A Life of Christopher Wren*. London: Jonathan Cape, 2001, p. 111.

Chapter 5

Page 46, line 5: *The Forgotten Genius*, p. 39.

Page 47, line 19: Ibid., p. 42.

Page 49, line 2: *England's Leonardo*, p. 101.

Page 51, line 12: Ibid., p. 81-82.

Page 52, line 8: *The Curious Life of Robert Hooke*, p. 115.

Page 52, line 18: Ibid., p. 117.

Page 52, line 26: *The Forgotten Genius*, p. 74.

Page 55, line 11: *Micrographia*, preface

Page 55, line 16: "January/February 1664–1665." *The Diary of Samuel Pepys*. Project Gutenberg Ebook, www.gutenberg.org/files/4154/4154.txt

Chapter 6

Page 57, line 7: *England's Leonardo*, p. 265.

Page 59, line 5: Henry W. Robinson, ed. *The Diary of Robert Hooke 1672–1680*. London: Wykeham Publications, 1963, p. 423.

Page 59, line 10: *The Forgotten Genius*, p. 46.

Page 60, line 19: *His Invention So Fertile*, p. 151.

Chapter 7

Page 69, line 12: James Gleick. *Isaac Newton*. New York: Pantheon Books, 2003, p. 98.

Page 70, line 6: *The Forgotten Genius*, p. 153.

Page 70, line 10: *Isaac Newton*, p. 87.

Page 74, line 8: *The Diary of Robert Hooke*, p. 192.

Page 75, line 7: Ibid., p. 157.

Page 76, line 13: Ibid., p. 172.

Chapter 8

Page 81, line 23: *Isaac Newton*, p. 117.

Page 84, line 7: *The Curious Life of Robert Hooke*, p. 6

Page 84, line 12: *Isaac Newton*, p. 127.

Page 85, line 1: Ibid.

Page 85, line 24: *The Curious Life of Robert Hooke*, p. 3.

Page 87, line 2: *The Forgotten Genius*, p. 2.

Page 87, line 24: *The Curious Life of Robert Hooke*, p. 258.

Chapter 9

Page 90, line 3: Ibid., p. 289–290.

Page 91, line 7: *The Forgotten Genius*, p. 367.

Page 92, line 24: Ibid., p. 402.

Page 93, line 9: Ibid., p. 409.

Page 93, line 14: Ibid., p. 307.

Select Bibliography

Chapman, Allan. *England's Leonardo: Robert Hooke and the Seventeenth-Century Scientific Revolution*. Bristol, England: Institute of Physics Publishing, 2005.

Chartres, Richard, and David Vermont. *A Brief History of Gresham College*. London: Gresham College, 1997. www.gresham.ac.uk/uploads/historygreshm_bk2.pdf

Gleick, James. *Isaac Newton*. New York: Pantheon Books, 2003.

Hooke, Robert. *Micrographia*. CD-Rom edition. Palo Alto, California: Octavo, 1998.

Inwood, Stephen. *The Forgotten Genius: The Biography of Robert Hooke 1635–1703*. San Francisco: MacAdam/Cake, 2003.

Jardine, Lisa. *The Curious Life of Robert Hooke: The Man Who Measured London*. New York: HarperCollins, 2004.

Nichols, Richard. *The Diaries of Robert Hooke, the Leonardo of London, 1635–1703*. Sussex, England: The Book Guild Ltd., 1994.

Tinniswood, Adrian. *His Invention So Fertile: A Life of Christopher Wren*. London: Jonathan Cape, 2001.

Windelspecht, Michael. *Groundbreaking Scientific Experiments, Inventions, & Discoveries of the 17th Century*. Westport, Conn.: Greenwood Press, 2002.

Michael Burgan is a freelance writer of books for children and adults. A history graduate of the University of Connecticut, he has written more than 100 fiction and nonfiction children's books. For adult audiences, he has written news articles, essays, and plays. Michael Burgan is a recipient of an Educational Press Association of America award.

Image Credits